Cursive Handwriting
Practice with

Tales & Legends

3 Classic Stories
Letters, Words, and Sentences

How to Use this Workbook:

Trace the letters, words, and sentences first, and then practice writing them in the remaining blank space.

Once they have mastered letters and how to connect letters, feel free to mix and match Parts II and III each day for practice. Combining rote practice with creativity will help maintain their enthusiasm as the story builds.

Each story page in Part III has a corresponding creative drawing page with prompts to inspire and excite your student's imagination. A "Talk about it" question is also included on most doodle drawing pages for reading comprehension, empathy building and emotional regulation, and growing the bond between teacher and student.

Helpful hint: For the reluctant writer, use the doodle pages as a reward at the end of a writing session.

Part I: Letter formation
Part II: Word building from short to long words
Part III: Story sentences, doodle pages, "talk about it" questions

Part One - Letter Formation

Aa Bb Cc Dd Ee

Ff Gg Hh Ii Jj

Kk Ll Mm Nn

Oo Pp Qq Rr Ss

Tt Uu Vv Ww

Xx Yy Zz

Aa Bb Cc Dd Ee Ff Gg Hh Ii Jj Kk Ll Mm Nn Oo Pp Qq Rr Ss Tt Uu Vv Ww Xx Yy Zz

Aa Bb Cc Dd Ee Ff Gg

Hh Ii Jj Kk Ll Mm Nn

Oo Pp Qq Rr Ss Tt Uu

Vv Ww Xx Yy Zz

My Name:

Aa Bb Cc Dd Ee Ff Gg
Hh Ii Jj Kk Ll Mm Nn
Oo Pp Qq Rr Ss Tt Uu
Vv Ww Xx Yy Zz

My Name:

Aa Bb Cc Dd Ee Ff Gg Hh Ii Jj Kk Ll Mm Nn Oo Pp Qq Rr Ss Tt Uu Vv Ww Xx Yy Zz

Part Two ~ Word Building

Aa Bb Cc Dd Ee Ff Gg Hh Ii Jj Kk Ll Mm Nn Oo Pp Qq Rr Ss Tt Uu Vv Ww Xx Yy Zz

Ch ch Ch ch

Sh sh Sh sh

Th th Th th

To to To to

In in In in

Of of Of of

It it It it

Is is Is is

Be be Be be

As as As as

Aa Bb Cc Dd Ee Ff Gg Hh Ii Jj Kk Ll Mm Nn Oo Pp Qq Rr Ss Tt Uu Vv Ww Xx Yy Zz

So so So so

We we We we

He he He he

By by By by

On on On on

Do do Do do

Me me Me me

Up up Up up

Go go Go go

No no No no

Aa Bb Cc Dd Ee Ff Gg Hh Ii Jj Kk Ll Mm Nn Oo Pp Qq Rr Ss Tt Uu Vv Ww Xx Yy Zz

Are are

And and

For for

Not not

But but

Had had

Was was

All all

One one

Man man

Aa Bb Cc Dd Ee Ff Gg Hh Ii Jj Kk Ll Mm Nn Oo Pp Qq Rr Ss Tt Uu Vv Ww Xx Yy Zz

Run run

Fly fly

Win win

Bold bold

Zeal zeal

Vast vast

Lost lost

Play play

King king

Jump jump

Aa Bb Cc Dd Ee Ff Gg Hh Ii Jj Kk Ll Mm Nn Oo Pp Qq Rr Ss Tt Uu Vv Ww Xx Yy Zz

Kind Kind

Girl girl

Have have

They they

Come come

Your your

Will will

From from

Once once

Hood hood

Aa Bb Cc Dd Ee Ff Gg Hh Ii Jj Kk Ll Mm Nn Oo Pp Qq Rr Ss Tt Uu Vv Ww Xx Yy Zz

Brave brave Brave

Pixie pixie Pixie pixie

Fight fight Fight fight

Truth truth Truth truth

Sword sword Sword

Aa Bb Cc Dd Ee Ff Gg Hh Ii Jj Kk Ll Mm Nn Oo Pp Qq Rr Ss Tt Uu Vv Ww Xx Yy Zz

Moral moral Moral

Crept crept Crept crept

Prince prince Prince

Battle battle Battle

Wizard wizard Wizard

Aa Bb Cc Dd Ee Ff Gg Hh Ii Jj Kk Ll Mm Nn Oo Pp Qq Rr Ss Tt Uu Vv Ww Xx Yy Zz

Aa Bb Cc Dd Ee Ff Gg Hh Ii Jj Kk Ll Mm Nn Oo Pp Qq Rr Ss Tt Uu Vv Ww Xx Yy Zz

Knight knight Knight

Weapon weapon

Wisdom wisdom

Family family Family

Honesty honesty

Aa Bb Cc Dd Ee Ff Gg Hh Ii Jj Kk Ll Mm Nn Oo Pp Qq Rr Ss Tt Uu Vv Ww Xx Yy Zz

Aa Bb Cc Dd Ee Ff Gg Hh Ii Jj Kk Ll Mm Nn Oo Pp Qq Rr Ss Tt Uu Vv Ww Xx Yy Zz

Magical magical

Camelot camelot

Kingdom kingdom

Pirates pirates

Indians indians

Aa Bb Cc Dd Ee Ff Gg Hh Ii Jj Kk Ll Mm Nn Oo Pp Qq Rr Ss Tt Uu Vv Ww Xx Yy Zz

Bedtime bedtime

Tyranny tyranny

Jealousy jealousy

Grateful grateful

Discover discover

Aa Bb Cc Dd Ee Ff Gg Hh Ii Jj Kk Ll Mm Nn Oo Pp Qq Rr Ss Tt Uu Vv Ww Xx Yy Zz

Persevere persevere

Crocodiles crocodiles

Neverland neverland

Kidnapped kidnapped

Protection protection

Aa Bb Cc Dd Ee Ff Gg Hh Ii Jj Kk Ll Mm Nn Oo Pp Qq Rr Ss Tt Uu Vv Ww Xx Yy Zz

Aa Bb Cc Dd Ee Ff Gg Hh Ii Jj Kk Ll Mm Nn Oo Pp Qq Rr Ss Tt Uu Vv Ww Xx Yy Zz

Character character

Dangerous dangerous

Prosperity prosperity

Happiness happiness

Adventure adventure

Aa Bb Cc Dd Ee Ff Gg Hh Ii Jj Kk Ll Mm Nn Oo Pp Qq Rr Ss Tt Uu Vv Ww Xx Yy Zz

Aa Bb Cc Dd Ee Ff Gg Hh Ii Jj Kk Ll Mm Nn Oo Pp Qq Rr Ss Tt Uu Vv Ww Xx Yy Zz

Treacherous treacherous

Tournament tournament

Circumstance

Relationships

Unfortunately

Aa Bb Cc Dd Ee Ff Gg Hh Ii Jj Kk Ll Mm Nn Oo Pp Qq Rr Ss Tt Uu Vv Ww Xx Yy Zz

My name is

I am   years old.

I live in

I like to

I don't like to

Part Three - Story Sentences

Peter Pan

Once upon a time, three children loved hearing bedtime stories about a boy from Neverland named Peter Pan.

Draw what you think Neverland looks like:

Wendy, John, and
Michael Darling begged
to hear about the boy
who never grew up,
pirates, and indians.

Draw a picture of your family:

Talk about it: Why do you think Peter Pan never grew up in Neverland?

Even Peter Pan himself
would fly to their
windowsill to listen.
One evening, he flew
them to Neverland!

**Imagine flying over your house to Neverland.
Draw what your house looks like down below:**

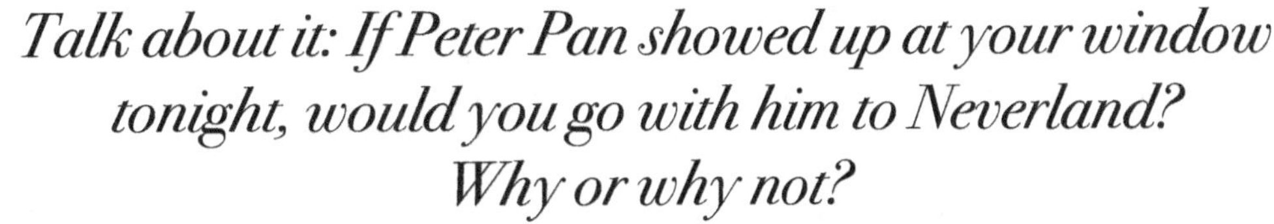

*Talk about it: If Peter Pan showed up at your window
tonight, would you go with him to Neverland?
Why or why not?*

With a bit of pixie dust
and a wish, they flew
to the Neverland. There
they met fairies, Lost
Boys, and indians.

Draw what you think Lost Boys, indians, and fairies looked like:

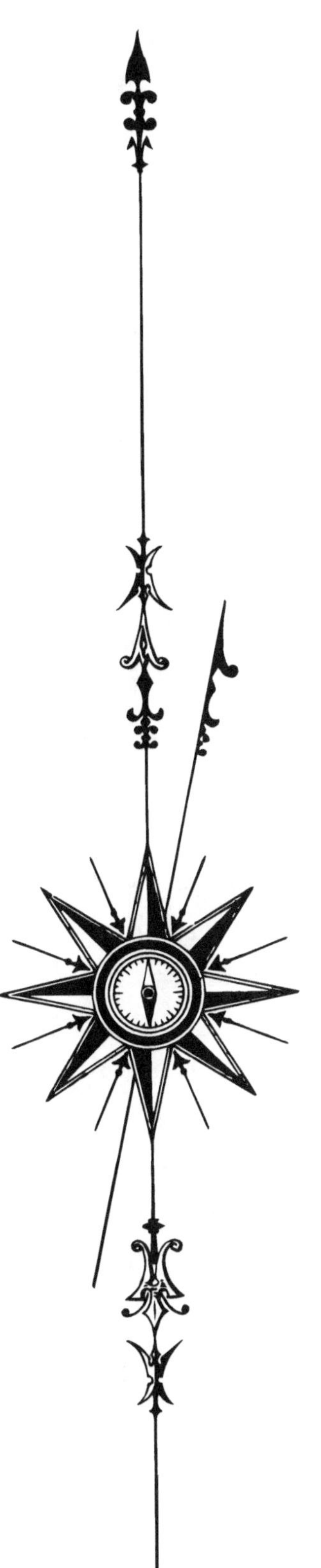

Talk about it: Which would you be most excited to meet- fairies, Lost Boys, or the indians? Why?

Unfortunately, they also met Captain Hook and his band of pirates. Hook and Pan were enemies always fighting.

Draw an epic battle between Peter Pan and Captain Hook:

Talk about it: Why do you think Captain Hook and Peter Pan were always fighting?

But the children loved
Neverland despite Hook.
After playing all day,
the Lost Boys adored
Wendy's bedtime stories.

**Draw what games you would play with the Lost Boys:
(remember, there are no grown-ups in Neverland!)**

*Talk about it: Why do you think the Lost Boys liked it
when Wendy told them bedtime stories?*

One day, the pirates
stole Princess Tiger Lily
of the red Indians!
Peter pan rescued her
which angered Hook.

Draw how you think the pirates kidnapped Princess Tiger Lily:

Talk about it: Why did Captain Hook kidnap Princess Tiger Lily?

Out of vengeance, Hook
kidnapped Pan's new
friends with a plan to
feed them to the large,
vicious crocodiles!

**Draw the meanest, hungriest crocodile
you can imagine:**

*Talk about it: How do you think Wendy, John, and
Michael felt? Why?*

As Wendy walked the plank to the crocodiles below, Peter Pan flew to save the day! He beat Hook once and for all!

Write about or draw how you think Peter Pan beat Captain Hook:

Talk about it: Do you think Peter Pan always feels brave? Why or why not?

All of Neverland was
free of Captain Hook's
tyranny. The pirates
were so afraid they
jumped overboard.

Draw the pirates jumping over the ship:

Talk about it: What do you think happened to the pirates?

The children loved
Neverland but they
missed home. With a
wish and some pixie
dust the ship flew home.

Draw the flying ship:

Talk about it: What would you have missed most about Neverland? Why?

The ship traveled back
to their home where
they grew up, unlike
the Lost Boys, but they
never forgot Peter Pan.

Write about or draw what you would miss from home the most if you visited Neverland:

Talk about it: Wendy, John, and Michael could have lived forever in Neverland! Why do you think they chose to come back home? What was missing?

Morals of the story: Relationships are worth sacrificing for. Also, happy thoughts can take you far.

Write about or draw your happiest thought:

Talk about it: What was your favorite part of the story?
Why?

Adapted from one of Howard Pyle's original stories found in "The Merry Adventures of Robin Hood"

Once upon a time,
wicked Prince John
ruled England while
good King Richard was
fighting in battle.

Draw a battle with brave knights' swords clashing:

Talk about it: What makes a King good or wicked?

Prince John was greedy
for money and power.
He set high taxes on the
people, forcing many to
become outlaws.

Draw what you want most in life:

Talk about it: Prince John hurt others to get what he wanted most. What kind of person do you think he is?

Not all outlaws were
dangerous or hurtful to
others. Robin Hood and
Little John did good
things for the people.

Draw something you do to help others:

Talk about it: What is an "outlaw?"

They were famous for
stealing from the rich,
who were profiting off
the high taxes, and
giving it to the poor.

Draw how you would feel if someone stole from you :

Talk about it: Is it ok to break the rules for a good reason? Why or why not?

They were clever with
their ruses and tricked
the rich traveling by
carriage through the
Sherwood Forest.

Draw what you think Sherwood Forest looked like:

One day, Prince John was passing through the forest collecting taxes. He was surrounded by bags of glittering gold.

Draw Prince John surrounded by all his gold:

Talk about it: When can having gold/money be a good thing?
When can it be a bad thing?

Robin Hood and
Little John dressed up
as lady fortune-tellers
beside the road, causing
the prince to stop.

Draw Robin Hood and Little John as lady fortune-tellers:

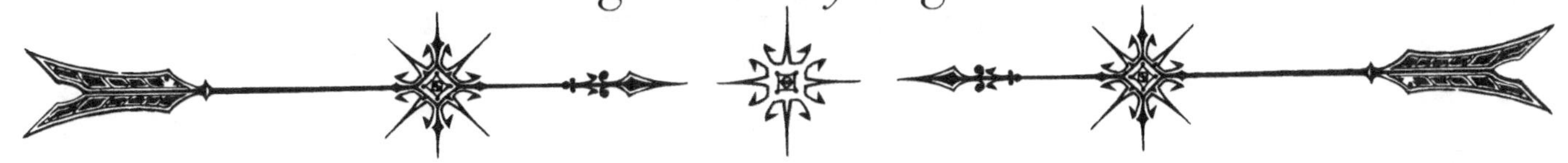

Talk about it: Do you think Prince John will recognize them through their silly disguises?!

While he was distracted
by his fortune being
told, they quickly stole
his bags of gold from
the empty carriage!

Write about or draw a time when you were tricked:

Talk about it: Tell me about what you wrote or drew. How did you feel when you discovered you had been tricked?

Prince John didn't
realize until they had
gotten far away. He
was furious and vowed
to avenge himself.

Draw Prince John's angriest face:

Talk about it: How do you think Prince John will avenge himself?

He teamed up with
Sheriff Nottingham,
who had his own
personal vendetta
against Robin Hood.

Draw the person you like to "team up" with:

*Talk about it: Why do you think Robin Hood had
so many enemies?*

Sheriff Nottingham plotted how to trap the notorious outlaw. He knew catching Robin Hood wouldn't be easy.

Draw how you would catch Robin Hood:

Talk about it: Tell me about what you drew. How do you think he could escape your plan?

He would have to lure
him with a contest and
the prize of a golden
arrow and kiss from
Maid Marian.

**Draw the prize that would make you want to
risk your life to have:**

Talk about it: Why did you choose what you chose to draw?

Maid Marian and
Robin Hood were old
sweethearts but her
parents would never let
her to marry an outlaw.

Draw something you would really like to have but you aren't allowed:

Talk about it: Why do you think it would be a bad idea to have it? What could go wrong?

Presently, she was unwillingly promised to an arrogant, greedy man. She was coming up with a plan to escape.

Draw how you think Maid Marian should escape from her castle:

Talk about it: Sometimes, we can't escape from our problems.
How can we learn to be content when we can't run away?

When she heard that
Robin Hood would
compete in the archery
contest, she put off her
plan of escape to see him.

Draw the type of contest you would want to compete in:

Talk about it: Do you think you would win that type of contest? Why or why not?

She was no fool. Robin
Hood was the best archer
in England and would
likely win. Her promised
kiss was meant for him.

Write about or draw a time when you won something:

Talk about it: How did it feel to win? How did it feel during the competition? Were those feelings different?

The day of Robin Hood
showed up in disguise
and won the archery
tournament! The prince
and sheriff were ready.

Draw how you would dress up to disguise yourself:

Talk about it: Why did you choose what you chose to draw?

As he accepted the prize,
a horn blew, and the
sheriff's men rushed to
seize him. Guards and
outlaws began to fight.

Draw something you would WANT to surround you:

Talk about it: How do you think Robin Hood felt when he saw guards surrounding him?

Little John took an
arrow to the knee, but
Robin Hood carried him
to safety in the forest.
Maid Marian followed.

Draw your best friend:

Talk about it: Do you think Little John regretted fighting alongside Robin Hood after getting shot with an arrow?

Prince John was furious
and punished the whole
kingdom by raising
taxes so high that nearly
everyone was made poor.

Write about or draw a time when you felt your life was unfair:

The sheriff even robbed
the church and threw
the priest in jail. Robin
Hood couldn't stand for
this cruel injustice.

Draw the jail full of people:

*Talk about it: How do you think the people felt about
Prince John and Sheriff Nottingham?*

He plotted how to free
the priest and help the
people before the priest
was hung in the early
morning by the prince.

Draw how you would help the people escape the prison:

Meanwhile, Prince John
and Sheriff Nottingham
planned to capture
Robin Hood when he
came to rescue the priest.

**Draw how you think the Prince and Sheriff will capture
Robin Hood this time:**

*Talk about it: Do you think this trap will work?
Why or why not?*

But Robin Hood was
clever and dressed as a
castle guard in the dark
of night. He quietly
broke into the castle.

Draw the items you would have taken with you to break into the castle and free the people:

*Talk about it: Why did he break in at night? Why did he dress
as a castle guard?*

The sheriff and prince
were sound asleep, so he
quickly stole the prison
keys and bags of gold
out from under them.

**Draw where you think Sheriff Nottingham
had kept the prison keys:**

*Talk about it: Why did he grab the bags of gold? Didn't he
only need the keys to free the people?*

He freed all the trapped prisoners, including the priest, and fled the castle with gold in hand and arrows chasing.

**Write about or draw a time when you were scared but
had to be brave:**

Talk about it: Tell me about what you wrote/drew.

King Richard finally
returned from battle
and lifted the heavy
taxes. He was angry
with the greedy prince.

Write about or draw a time when you let someone borrow something and they mistreated or broke it:

Talk about it: How did you feel when you got the item back?
Did you still trust them with your things afterwards?

Happiness and prosperity
returned to the land,
but Robin Hood, friends,
and Marian stayed
gladly in the forest.

Draw what you think Robin Hood's home looked like in the Sherwood Forest:

Talk about it: Why do you think Robin Hood, his friends, and Maid Marian stayed in the forest when they could have moved back to the city?

Morals of the story:
Never be afraid to stand
up to injustice. It is
better to serve others
than yourself.

Draw your favorite part of the story:

Talk about it: Was Robin Hood a hero or a villain? Why?

Adapted from T.H. White's original story, "The Sword in the Stone"

Arthur and his father,
the King of Camelot,
loved each other very
much. He was raised to
be honest and good.

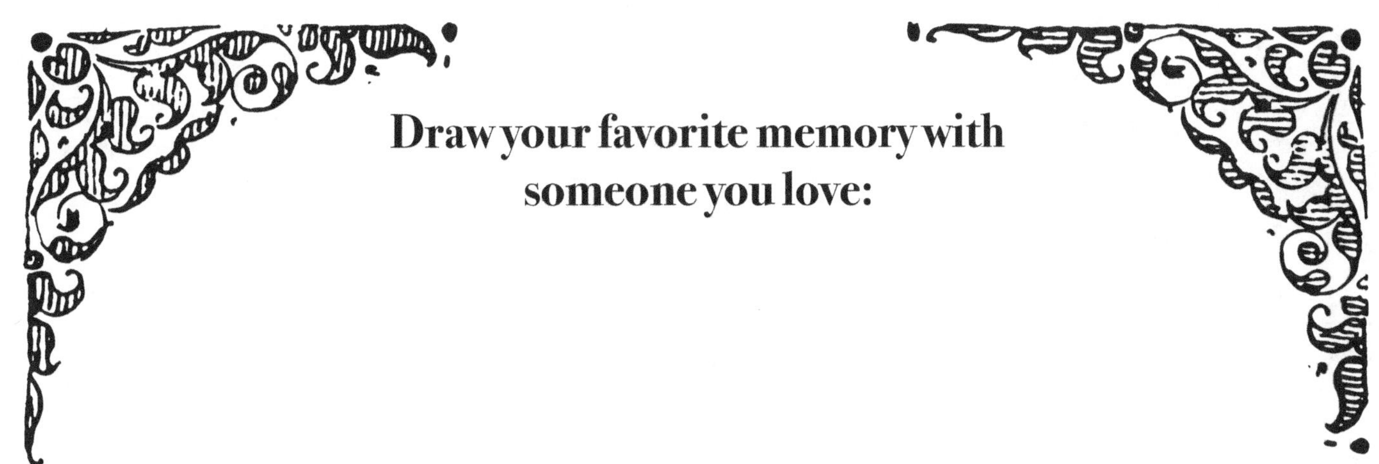

**Draw your favorite memory with
someone you love:**

*Talk about it: Why is it important for the future
king to be good and honest?*

Unfortunately, other
kings were jealous and
wanted Camelot so they
schemed to kill Arthur
and take the throne.

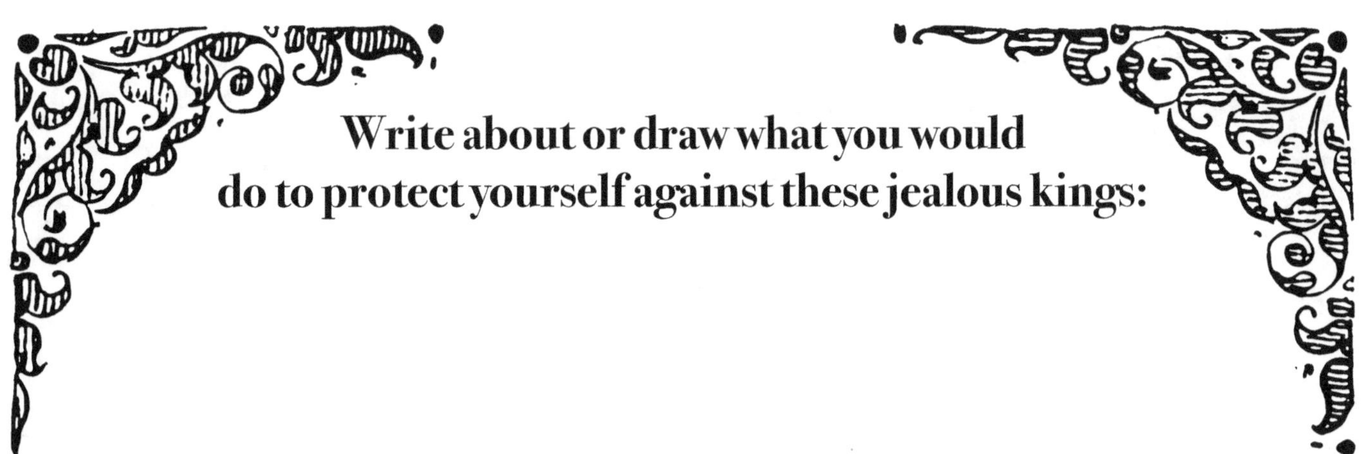

Write about or draw what you would
do to protect yourself against these jealous kings:

Talk about it: Have you ever been jealous of something
someone else had? What's a healthy way to deal
with these feelings?

To protect his son and
kingdom, the King sent
Arthur away with
Merlin the Wizard and
the knight, Sir Ector.

**Draw what you think Merlin the Wizard
or Sit Ector the Knight looked like:**

*Talk about it: Why do you think the King chose
these specific men to protect Arthur?*

With Merlin's magical
protection and Sir Ector
teaching him the ways
of a king, he was well-
raised but missed by all.

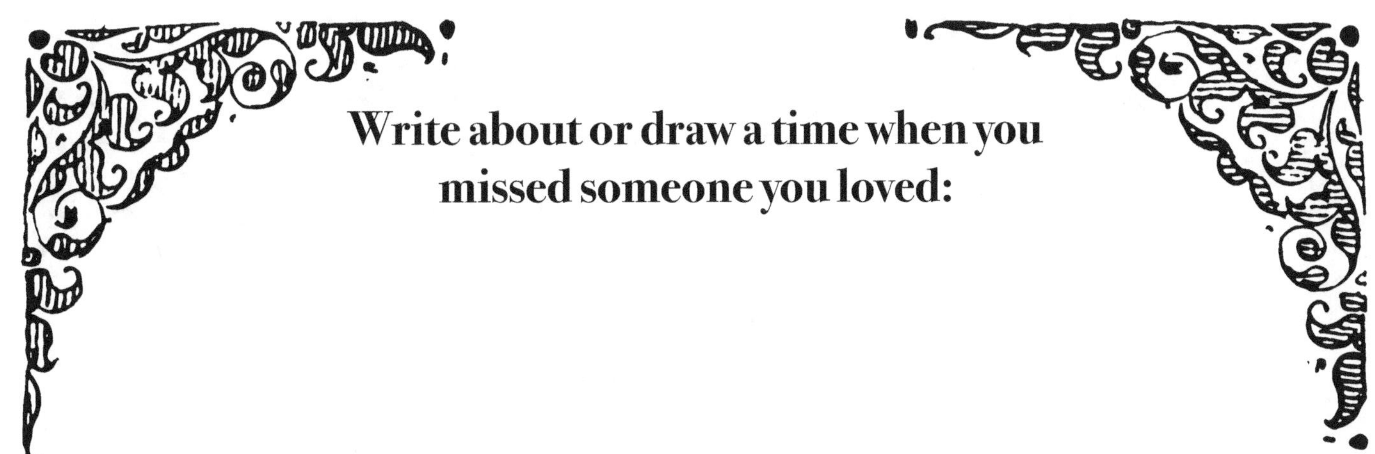

**Write about or draw a time when you
missed someone you loved:**

*Talk about it: Tell me about what you wrote/
drew. What can we do when we miss someone?*

When his father died,
there were riots and
famine in Camelot as
the nobles argued who
would become the king.

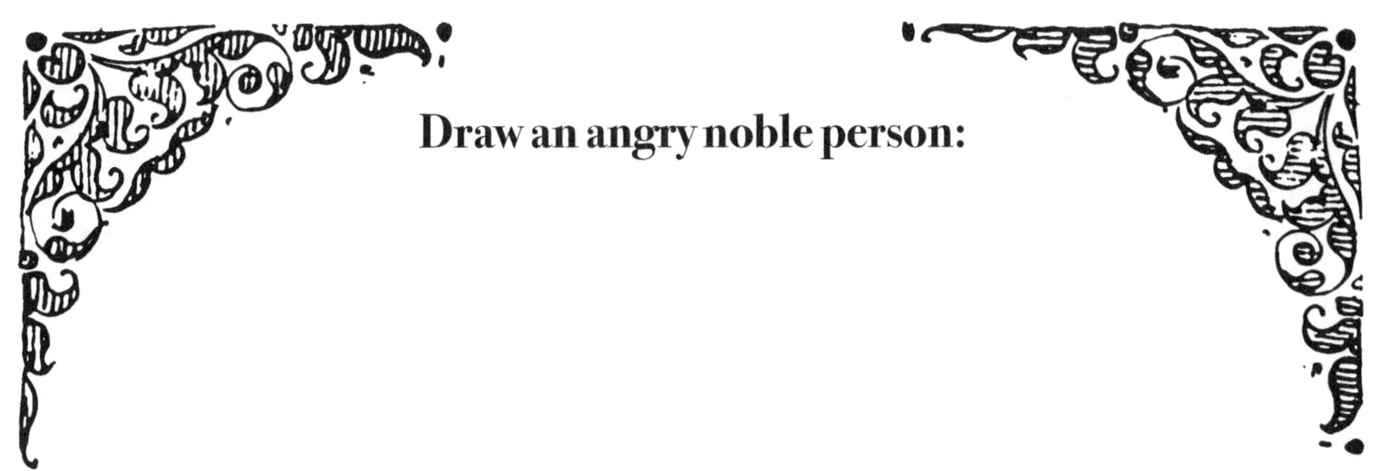

Draw an angry noble person:

*Talk about it: How would YOU stop the nobles
from arguing if you were in charge?*

To give Arthur more time, Merlin made a sword in a stone that could only be removed by the next true king.

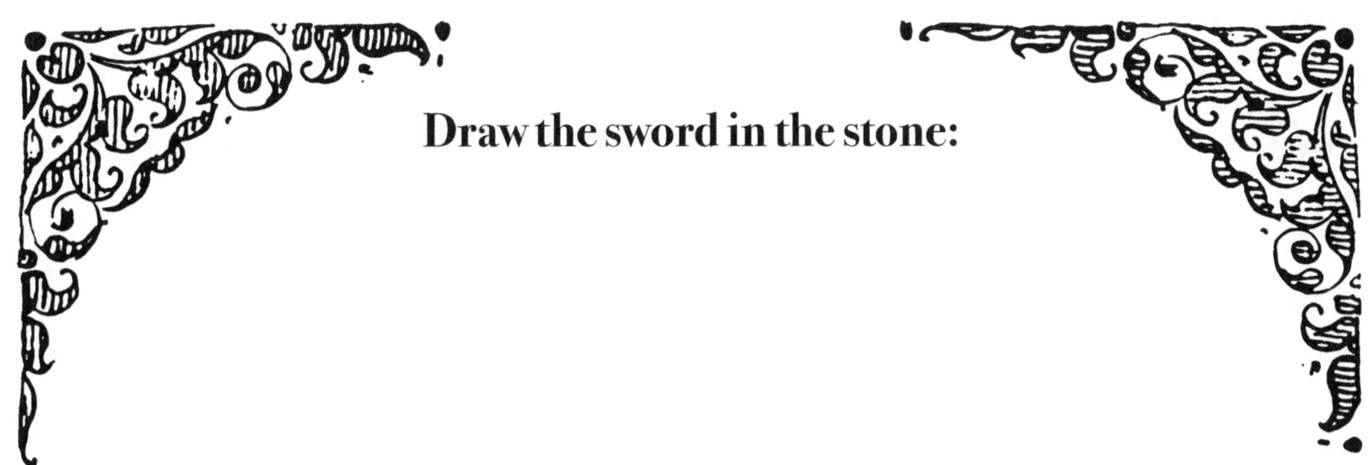

Draw the sword in the stone:

*Talk about it: Do you think you could remove
the sword? Why or why not?*

All the nobles tried to
remove the sword but
failed. The kingdom
continued to starve and
fight one another.

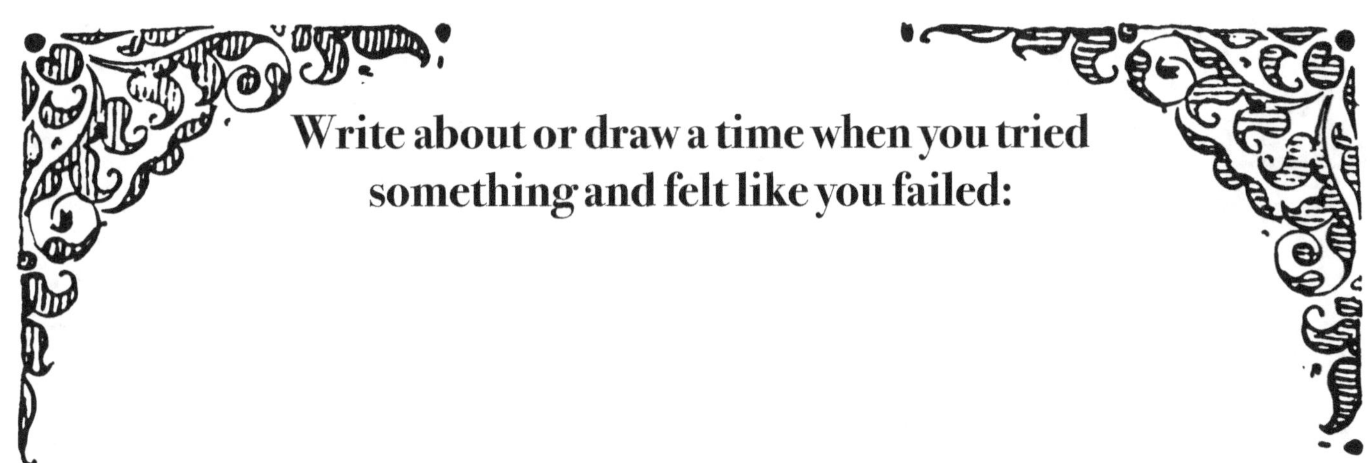

Write about or draw a time when you tried something and felt like you failed:

Talk about it: What does it mean to fail something? If you learned something from it, do you still call it a failure?

After years of misery,
Arthur was still small
in size but old enough
to try to release the
sword from the stone.

*Talk about it: Have you ever felt too small to do something
great? Tell me about it.*

At first he tried and failed! How could someone so weak be king? The crowd laughed and mocked him.

Write about or draw a time when you or someone else was made fun of for trying something new:

Talk about it: What would you tell Arthur after everyone laughed at him for trying?

Merlin tells him his
strength is in his kind,
wise, and honest heart.
His inner strength will
release the sword.

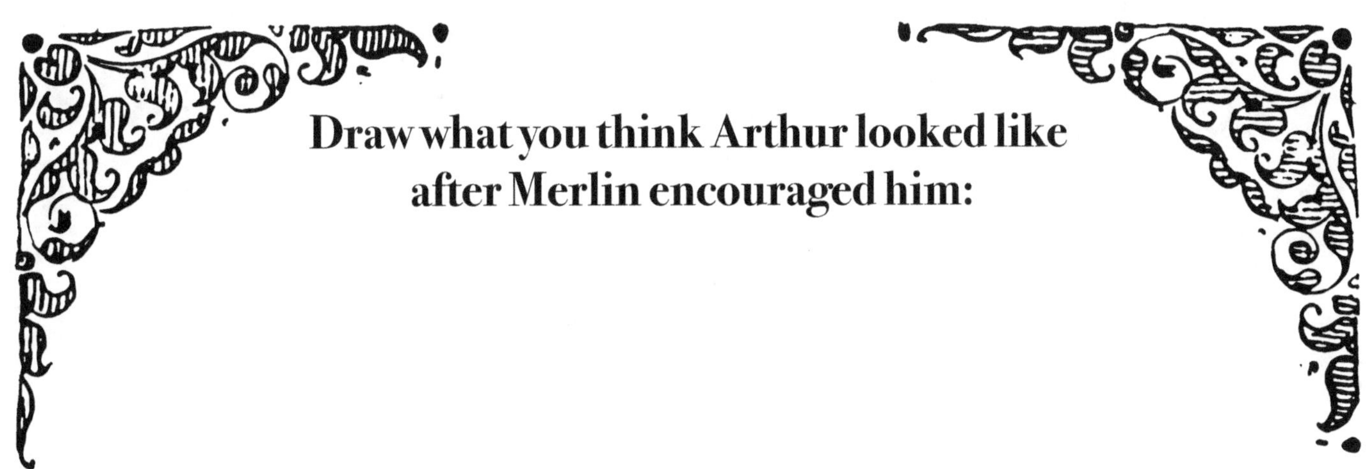

**Draw what you think Arthur looked like
after Merlin encouraged him:**

Arthur tried again
despite the crowd's jeers.
They were amazed as the
sword slid out revealing
Arthur as king!

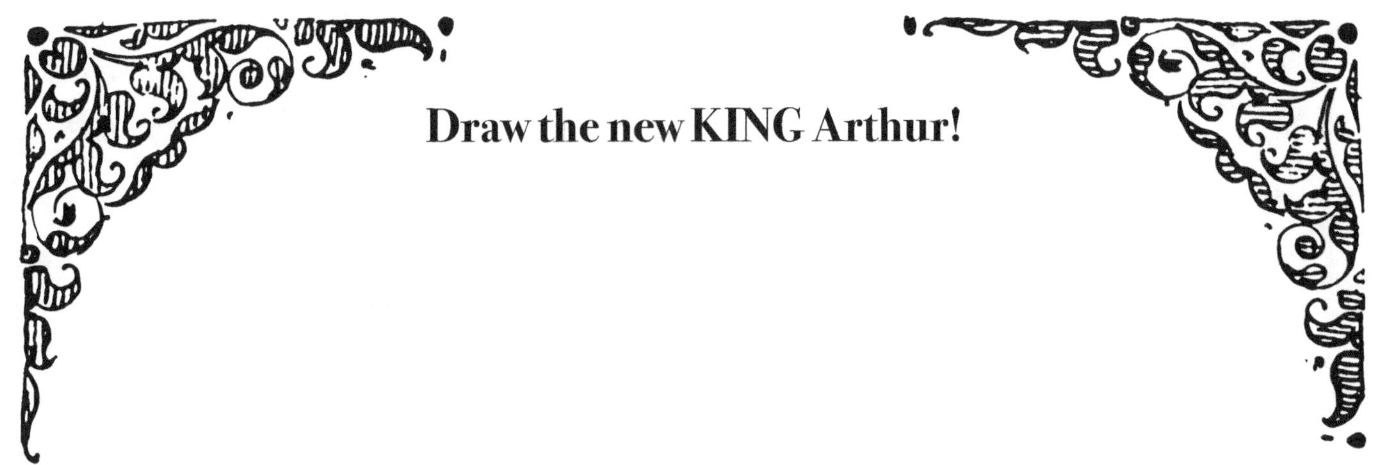

Draw the new KING Arthur!

Talk about it: What changed from the last time Arthur tried to pull the sword out? Why did this time work?

King Arthur was a
mighty king who led
with the heart, bravery,
and wisdom shown the
day he pulled the sword.

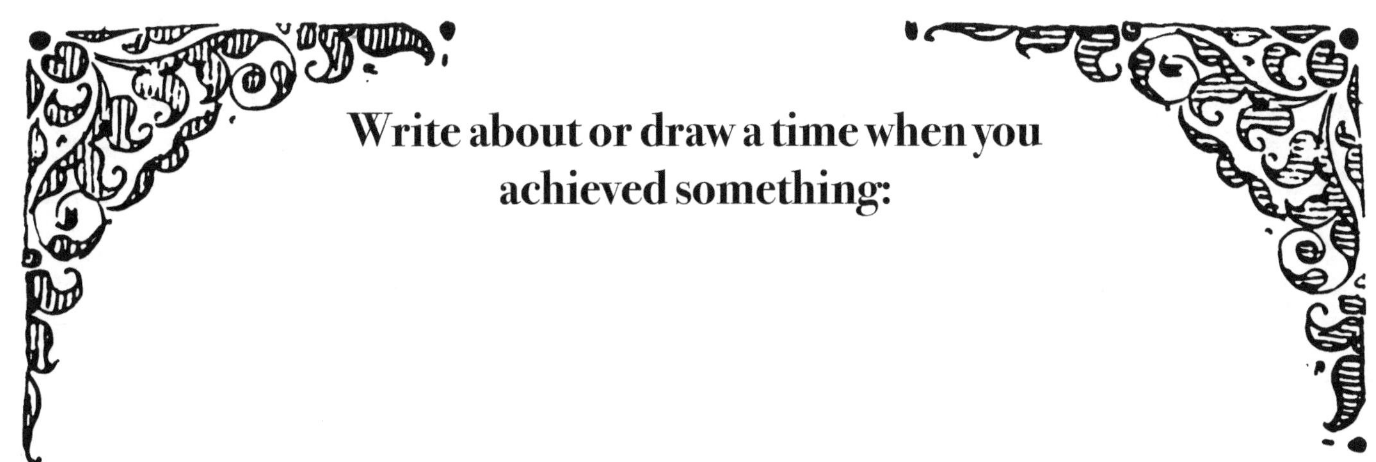

**Write about or draw a time when you
achieved something:**

*Talk about it: How can we have a heart of bravery, honesty,
and wisdom like King Arthur?*

Moral of the story:
Who you are and what
you have inside matters
more than what you
look like on the outside.

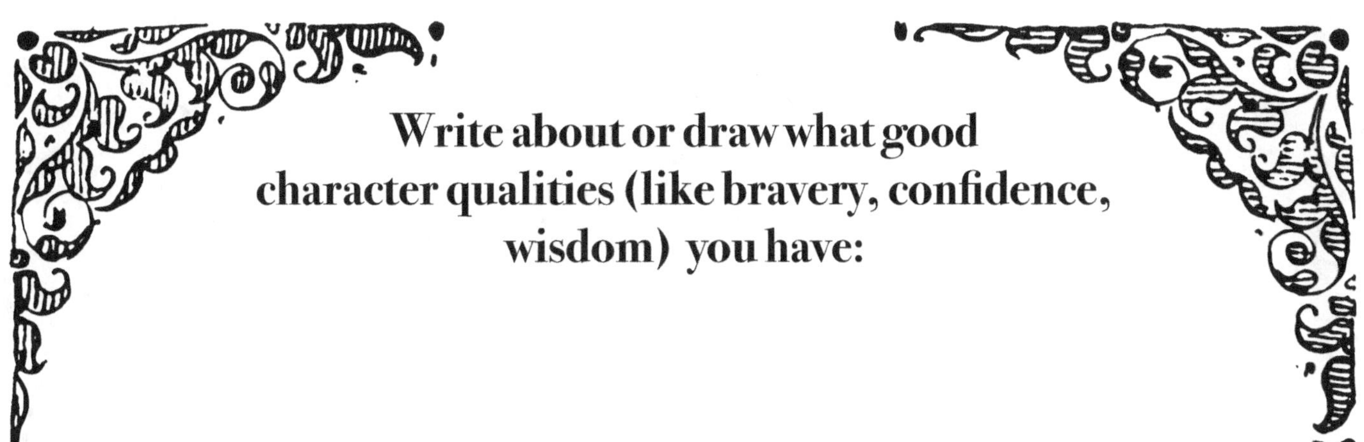

Write about or draw what good character qualities (like bravery, confidence, wisdom) you have:

Talk about it: How can we choose to use our good character qualities when we really don't want to or are afraid?